O9-BTJ-866

This Book
Belongs to

_____

_____

The Easter Story

ISBN-13: 978-0-8249-5531-1
ISBN-10: 0-8249-5531-5

Published by WorthyKids/Ideals
An imprint of Worthy Publishing Group
A division of Worthy Media, Inc.
Nashville, Tennessee

Copyright © 2006 by Ideals Publications

All rights reserved. No part of this publication may be reproduced or transmitted in any
form or by any means, electronic or mechanical, including photocopy, recording, or any
information storage and retrieval system, without permission in writing from the publisher.

WorthyKids/Ideals is a registered trademark of Worthy Media, Inc.

Library of Congress CIP data on file

Color separations by Precision Color Graphics, Franklin, Wisconsin

Printed and bound in China

RRD-SZ_ Oct16_13

 For Abigail

The Easter Story

By Patricia A. Pingry

Illustrated by Mary Ann Utt

WorthyKids
ideals®
Nashville, Tennessee

When
we celebrate
Easter, we
remember
that God gave
us his Son,
Jesus Christ,
to be our
Savior.

Jesus made sick people well. He even made the dead live again!

Jesus chose
twelve men
to be his
disciples.
He told them
that God loves
us so much
that he sent
Jesus to die
for us.

But some people didn't want to hear about God. They didn't want to listen to Jesus.

On Palm Sunday, Jesus rode into Jerusalem. People shouted, "Hosanna to our King!"

Later, Jesus and his disciples ate the Passover supper. Jesus washed their feet to show how much he loved them.

After supper, they went to a garden to pray. But the men who didn't like Jesus sent soldiers to arrest him.

Jesus was sent to die. His disciples were very sad. But Jesus had told them that he would rise after three days.

On the third day, women went to Jesus' tomb. The tomb was open. Jesus was not there!

That night,
Jesus' disciples
were in a
locked room.
Suddenly, Jesus
was there. He
was alive!

Jesus said, "Go and tell everyone that if a person believes in me, they will be saved. And they will live forever."

This is the
Easter Story,
that Jesus is
alive today.
And because
he died for
us, we will
live too.